PLANET EARTH
FACTS & LISTS

PLANET EARTH
FACTS & LISTS

Phillip Clarke

**Designed by Karen Tomlins,
Michael Hill, Adam Constantine**

Digital imagery by Keith Furnival

Consultant: Dr Roger Trend
Senior Lecturer in Earth Science
and Geography Education,
University of Exeter

Internet Links

Throughout this book, we have suggested interesting websites where you can find out more about Planet Earth. To visit the sites, go to the **Usborne Quicklinks website** at **www.usborne-quicklinks.com** and type the keywords "earth facts". There you will find links to click on to take you to all the sites. Here are some of the things you can do on the websites:

• Watch a volcano through a live webcam

• Explore the wonders of Planet Earth in an interactive atlas

• Try your hand at building an earthquake-proof skyscraper

Site availability

The links in **Usborne Quicklinks** are regularly reviewed and updated, but occasionally you may get a message that a site is unavailable. This might be temporary, so try again later, or even the next day. If any of the sites close down, we will, if possible, replace them with suitable alternatives, so you will always find an up-to-date list of sites in **Usborne Quicklinks**.

Internet safety

When using the Internet, please make sure you follow these guidelines:

• Ask your parent's or guardian's permission before you connect to the Internet.

• If you write a message in a website guest book or on a website message board, do not include any personal information such as your full name, address or telephone number, and ask an adult before you give your email address.

• If a website asks you to log in or register by typing your name or email address, ask permission from an adult first.

• If you receive an email from someone you don't know, tell an adult and do not reply to the email.

• Never arrange to meet anyone you have talked to on the Internet.

Note for parents and guardians

The websites described in this book are regularly reviewed and the links in **Usborne Quicklinks** are updated. However, the content of a website may change at any time and Usborne Publishing is not responsible for the content on any website other than its own.

We recommend that children are supervised while on the Internet, that they do not use Internet Chat Rooms, and that you use Internet filtering software to block unsuitable material. Please ensure that your children read and follow the safety guidelines printed on the left. For more information, see the **Net Help** area on the **Usborne Quicklinks** website.

Computer not essential

If you don't have access to the Internet, don't worry. This book is complete on its own.

Contents

Planet Earth

From out in space, the Earth looks like a small blue and green marble – yet it is home to over six billion people. There are trillions of stars in space, but we only know of a hundred or so planets, and Earth is the only one that we know for sure has life.

The Earth circles a star called the Sun. Scientists think that the Sun, Earth and our neighbouring planets were all made at the same time, about 4,600 million years ago.

Right now, you are spinning at around 1,600kph. This is how quickly the Earth spins. It's also travelling around the Sun at 105,000kph. The Milky Way itself turns at 900,000kph. Feeling dizzy?

The Sun is just one of over 200,000 million stars in our galaxy, the Milky Way. There are over 6,000 million galaxies in the universe.

YOU ARE HERE
The Sun is just one star in our huge galaxy... Feeling small?

Round trip

It takes 28 days for the Moon to travel around the Earth. It takes a whole year for the Earth to travel around the Sun.

Earth

Moon

Sun

The Moon is about a quarter the size of the Earth.

Earth's statistics

Diameter	
at the Poles	12,714km
at the equator	12,756km
Circumference	
around Poles	39,942km
around equator	40,075km
Density	5.515g/cm³
Volume	1.1 million million km³
Total surface area	510 million km²
Mass	6,000 million million million tonnes

North and south

Four out of five people on Earth live in the northern half of the planet. More of the southern half is covered in sea.

The biggest ocean, the Pacific, is three times the size of the biggest continent, Asia.

Continent	Area (km²)
Asia	44,537,920
Africa	30,311,690
North America	22,656,190
South America	17,866,130
Antarctica	13,340,000
Europe	10,205,720
Oceania	8,564,400

The Pacific Ocean covers a third of the Earth.

INTERNET LINKS
To find links to websites about Planet Earth go to **www.usborne-quicklinks.com**

Isolated isles

Bouvet Island in the Atlantic Ocean is the most isolated island on Earth. It is 1,600km from Africa and no one lives there. The most isolated lived-on island is Tristan da Cunha, 1,500km from Africa.

Africa

Tristan da Cunha
Bouvet Island

Largest islands	Area (km²)
Greenland	2,175,600
New Guinea	800,000
Borneo	751,100
Madagascar	587,040
Baffin Island, Canada	507,451
Sumatra, Indonesia	437,607
Honshu, Japan	230,455
Great Britain	229,870

7

At the Earth's Core

The Earth's rocky surface is called the crust. Under the oceans, the crust is 6km thick. Crust that makes up land is more like 40km thick. This may sound very thick, but if the Earth was an apple, its crust would only be as thick as the apple skin.

Earth's layers	Depth (km)	Temperature	Main content
Oceanic crust	6	500°C*	Basalt
Continental crust	40	500°C*	Granite
Mantle (radius)	2,870	1,500–3,000°C	Peridotite
Outer core (radius)	2,100	3,900°C	Liquid iron/nickel
Inner core (radius)	1,370	6,000°C	Solid iron/nickel

*This is the average temperature. It is 21°C near the surface.

The crust sits on a thicker layer of rock called the mantle. The rock here is hot enough to melt, but huge pressure squeezes it into a slow-moving solid.

Core blimey

The very middle of the Earth is called the core. It is thought to have an outer layer of liquid metal with a solid inner core – but of course no one's been there to check.

Scientists believe that the Earth's solid core is a huge iron crystal. Digging down to it would take a while though, as it lies more than 4,800km below the Earth's surface.

Layer upon layer

Geologists – scientists who study the Earth's structure – divide its crust and mantle into more layers:

Lithosphere
The rigid outer layer of the Earth, about 100km thick, made up of the crust and upper part of the mantle. Floats on the...

Asthenosphere
A hot, semi-liquid layer of the mantle, which is about 200km thick.

Crust

Inner core

Mantle

Outer core

How do they know?

Geologists have lots of ways of finding out about the Earth's insides:

Drilling

The Kola Superdeep Borehole in Russia is the world's deepest borehole, at 12.3km; yet it still only scratches the Earth's surface.

The deeper you drill into the crust, the older are the rocks. At the bottom of the Kola hole, rock dates back 2,800 million years – not long after the first plants appeared on Earth.

Earthquakes

Studying the paths of shockwaves caused by earthquakes has led geologists to believe that the Earth's outer core is liquid, while its mantle and inner core are solid.

Meteorites

Asteroids are rocks out in space. They are thought to be left over from when the planets formed and to be made of the same stuff. Meteorites are pieces of asteroid that fall to Earth. Studying these helps geologists work out what types of rock are hidden deep inside our own planet.

Monster magnet

Our planet is a huge magnet. Its magnetism is thought to be caused by its liquid outer core swirling around the inner core. If you've used a compass, you'll have seen Earth's magnetism at work. Compasses, though, don't point to the true North Pole, as the Earth's magnetic poles wander slowly over thousands of years. Navigators need to know how far apart the true and magnetic poles are to use maps accurately.

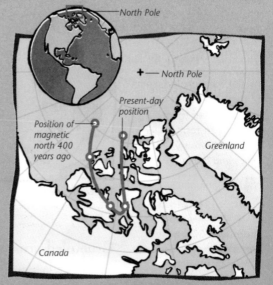

The Earth's magnetic poles slowly wander around the globe, even switching places completely every 250,000 years or so.

INTERNET LINKS
To find links to websites about the inside of the Earth, go to **www.usborne-quicklinks.com**

Scientists used to think the Earth was hollow and could be entered through holes at the Poles. In 1838, a group went to find the way in at the South Pole. They didn't find a hole, but did find land. This proved that Antarctica was more than just a frozen sea.

The Changing Earth

Scientists think that the Earth was made 4,600 million years ago from a spinning cloud of dust and gas. The cloud shrank into hot, molten balls.

Earth started life as a great ball of fire.

As the balls cooled, some of them hardened and gravity pulled them together to form rocky planets: Mercury, Venus, Mars and Earth.

The Moon was probably formed 4,500 million years ago, after a cosmic collision between the Earth and another planet the size of Mars. Rocky rubble from the crash exploded outwards and gradually formed the Moon you see today.

The Moon may once have been part of the Earth.

Giant jigsaw

Earth's outer shell isn't a single piece. It is broken into smaller pieces called tectonic plates. These drift on top of a semi-liquid layer in the Earth's mantle*. Oceanic (undersea) plates are much thinner than continental (land-bearing) plates.

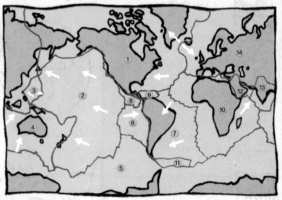

The Earth's plates   *Direction of drift*

1. North American
2. Pacific
3. Philippine
4. Australian
5. Antarctic
6. Nazca
7. South American
8. Cocos
9. Caribbean
10. African
11. Scotia
12. Arabian
13. Indian
14. Eurasian

Crumpled crust

As plates drift, they collide and crumple. Continental plates that meet buckle upwards to form mountain ranges. Tibet, for example, has risen over 3km in the last two million years. Oceanic plates plunge beneath continental plates, forming deep ocean trenches.

Slip sliding away

When plates slide past each other, they form big cracks, called faults. The San Andreas Fault, in the USA, stretches for over 1,000km through California to Mexico. Over 15 million years, western California has moved 300km north-west.

Part of the San Andreas Fault

*See page 8

Mountain high

The longest mountain range, the Mid-Atlantic Ridge, is under the sea. It is 11,000km long. It forms where liquid rock wells up between plates, cooling to form new rock.

Iceland is part of the Mid-Atlantic Ridge that rises above sea level.

Millions of years ago, North Africa was covered in ice and Antarctica was covered in rainforest. The Earth's plates drift, so even continents don't always stay in the same place.

Once upon a time in Antarctica...

Continental drift

Earth's plates drift no faster than your nails grow. But over millions of years, this slow movement can dramatically change the layout of the continents and oceans.

200 million years ago

200 million years ago, most of the Earth's land was joined in one huge continent, called Pangaea.

50 million years ago

50 million years ago, the land began to form the continents we know today.

50 million years from now?

As the plates continue to drift, Earth may one day look like this.

INTERNET LINKS
To find links to websites about the Earth's formation, and its plates, go to **www.usborne-quicklinks.com**

When plates collide

The boundaries between plates have names describing how the plates affect each other and what happens to the landscape when they meet.

Plate boundary		Landscape
Constructive: *Plates pull apart; magma (liquid rock) wells up and cools to form new crust.*		Spreading ridge, for example, the Mid-Atlantic Ridge
Destructive: *One plate dives under another, and melts back into mantle.*		Ocean trench, for example, the Mariana Trench (see *Undersea landscape*, page 43)
Conservative: *Plates rub past each other, causing earthquakes.*		Transform fault, for example, the San Andreas Fault

Earth's Atmosphere

The Earth is wrapped in a blanket of air called the atmosphere. The atmosphere is made up of several different layers. The highest layer stretches up into space, 8,000km above Earth.

Flying high

All the weather happens in the troposphere – the layer of atmosphere that hugs the Earth's surface. This is the only layer that contains enough water vapour to make clouds.

Big thunder clouds have flat tops where they hit the next layer of the atmosphere.

If all the water in the atmosphere fell in one massive downpour, it would cover the Earth's surface with 2.5cm of water.

2.5cm —

Mesosphere	50–80km	10°C to -80°C
Stratosphere	8–50km	-55°C to 10°C
Troposphere		
Height over equator 16km	*At 16km*	-55°C
Height over Poles 8km	*At sea level*	15°C

Gasping for air

The higher you go, the less air there is and the dizzier you get. This is why some mountaineers carry extra oxygen to breathe. The amount of oxygen at the top of Everest is just a third of the amount at sea level.

This mountaineer is climbing Mount Everest with the help of an oxygen mask.

Gases in the air

Nitrogen	78.0%
Oxygen	21.0%
Argon	0.9%
Carbon dioxide	0.03%
Other gases	0.07%

e.g. neon, helium, krypton, hydrogen, xenon, ozone

Radio waves

Radio waves move at the speed of light (300,000km per second). The signals travel around the curve of the Earth by bouncing off tiny particles in the atmosphere.

Troposphere
Stratosphere
Mesosphere
Thermosphere

Radio waves bounce back.

INTERNET LINKS
To find links to websites about the Earth's atmosphere, go to www.usborne-quicklinks.com

Breathe easy

The oxygen on Earth is 3,000 million years old. It began forming when simple, plant-like cells, called blue-green bacteria, appeared on the Earth. Plants in sunlight make oxygen, which all animals, including us, need to breathe.

Blue-green bacteria – tiny oxygen factories

Sun screen

The Sun isn't just a life-giver. It has damaging rays as well. High up in the stratosphere is a layer of ozone gas. Luckily for us, this filters out most of them.

Without the ozone layer to protect us from harmful ultraviolet rays, there would be no life on Earth.

A big volcanic eruption can throw dust and ash up into the stratosphere. This can travel halfway across the world and take up to three years to fall back to Earth.

Mount St Helens spouting ash

Height records

Vehicle	Height
Space Shuttle	623.6km
Unmanned balloon	53.0km
Mig-25 fighter plane	38.0km
Manned balloon	35.0km
Concorde	19.0km
Boeing-747 Jumbo jet	13.0km
DC-10 plane	12.2km

For comparison, Mount Everest is 8.9km high

Ozone layer

Rocks

Rocks are pieces of the Earth's crust. There are three main types:

Igneous rocks form when liquid rock, called magma, rises from the mantle, cools and becomes solid.

Sedimentary rocks are made from mud, sand or other stuff, called sediment, that has been squashed down into layers over millions of years. You can find fossils in this type of rock.

Metamorphic rocks are made from other rocks that have been changed by the massive pressure and heat inside the Earth. *Metamorphic* is from the Greek words for "changed shape".

Granite A hard, coarse-grained rock formed beneath the crust. Coloured pink to grey. It makes up most of the continental crust.

Chalk A soft rock, usually white; contains shells, and plant and animal remains.

Slate Formed from shale (a fine-grained sedimentary rock) under high pressure. Splits easily into thin sheets.

Basalt A hard, fine-grained rock formed in lava* flows. It is younger than granite and makes up most of the oceanic crust.

Limestone A hard rock; often contains many shells; usually white to grey, but may be red or honey-coloured.

Marble Formed from limestone warped by heat

Obsidian A black or greenish natural glass made when lava cools very quickly above ground in a volcanic eruption.

Sandstone A rock formed from the sands of beaches, rivers or deserts.

Quartzite Formed from sandstone changed by high pressure and heat

! Stones can float – at least, a pumice stone can. This is because it's full of trapped gas bubbles. It is an igneous rock made when lava cools quickly in a volcanic explosion.

INTERNET LINKS
To find out how to start your own rock collection, identify rocks, watch a cartoon history of the Earth, play some rocking online games and more besides, go to **www.usborne-quicklinks.com**

*Lava is magma flowing above the ground or seabed.

Rock recycling

Over millions of years, natural forces above and inside the Earth change rocks from one type into another.

Key

1 Igneous rock is formed as magma, rising from the mantle, cools.
2 Wind, rain and rivers wear away bare igneous rock. Pieces of sediment are carried to the sea.
3 Sediment settles on the seafloor. Over many years, it is packed into rock layers.
4 Heat and pressure under the Earth turns igneous and sedimentary rock into metamorphic rock.
5 Metamorphic rock melts back into the mantle.

Rock	Uses
Clay	Bricks. Paper making
Coal	Fuel
Feldspar	Porcelain making
Granite	Building
Limestone	Building. Steelmaking
Marble	Decorative stonework
Sandstone	Building

Boulders in Racetrack Playa, Death Valley, USA, have a strange habit of sliding around, leaving tracks behind. No one sees them move. They are thought to be nudged by wind across the flat plain when it's wet and slippery after rain.

Fossils

The remains or shapes of living things that died long ago can be found in sedimentary rock. The original remains have usually rotted away, but they may be replaced with sediment or minerals which hold the shape together.

This fossil is the remains of a prehistoric shellfish.

This rock formation in Arizona, USA, is made from prehistoric sand dunes that were slowly squeezed together.

Minerals

Minerals are made in the Earth. Rocks are made up of different types of minerals. The chart below shows the main types of minerals that can be found in the Earth's crust.

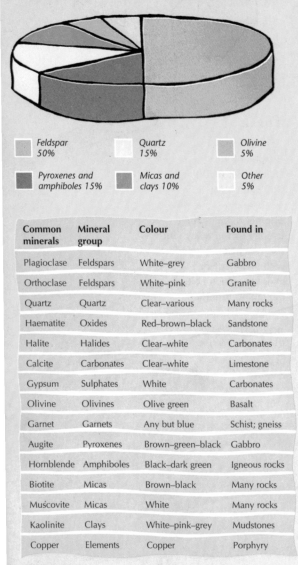

- Feldspar 50%
- Quartz 15%
- Olivine 5%
- Pyroxenes and amphiboles 15%
- Micas and clays 10%
- Other 5%

Common minerals	Mineral group	Colour	Found in
Plagioclase	Feldspars	White–grey	Gabbro
Orthoclase	Feldspars	White–pink	Granite
Quartz	Quartz	Clear–various	Many rocks
Haematite	Oxides	Red–brown–black	Sandstone
Halite	Halides	Clear–white	Carbonates
Calcite	Carbonates	Clear–white	Limestone
Gypsum	Sulphates	White	Carbonates
Olivine	Olivines	Olive green	Basalt
Garnet	Garnets	Any but blue	Schist; gneiss
Augite	Pyroxenes	Brown–green–black	Gabbro
Hornblende	Amphiboles	Black–dark green	Igneous rocks
Biotite	Micas	Brown–black	Many rocks
Muscovite	Micas	White	Many rocks
Kaolinite	Clays	White–pink–grey	Mudstones
Copper	Elements	Copper	Porphyry

Rock recipe

This close-up view of granite shows the minerals that make it up.

Plagioclase feldspar
Quartz
Orthoclase feldspar
Biotite mica

Mineral ID

Scientists identify minerals by the following:

Colour

Impurities in minerals make colours vary.

Traces of iron turn clear quartz into purple amethyst.

Streak

A mineral's colour may vary, but the streak it makes usually stays the same.

Haematite makes a red streak.

Lustre

The way a mineral shines

Citrine has a glassy lustre.

Cleavage

The way a mineral breaks

Some minerals break into sheets…   *…others break into blocks.*

Hardness

(See the Mohs scale opposite.)

Mohs hardness scale

A mineral can scratch those rated below it in this scale.

Hardness	Scratched by
1 Talc	Fingernail, easily
2 Gypsum	Fingernail
3 Calcite	Knife, very easily
4 Fluorite	Knife, easily
5 Apatite	Knife, just
	Scratches
6 Orthoclase	Glass, just
7 Quartz	Glass, easily
8 Topaz	Glass, very easily
9 Corundum	Cuts glass
10 Diamond	Corundum

Seeing double

If you look through a crystal of Iceland Spar, you will see a double image. Iceland Spar is a type of calcite. As rays of light pass through it, it splits them in two.

You'll look twice at Iceland Spar.

Glow stones

Some minerals can give off light. Fluorite glows blue if it's placed under ultraviolet light. This effect is called "fluorescence", after the mineral.

Quartz glowing red and fluorite glowing blue in ultraviolet light.

Cool crystals

When magma cools it usually forms into regular, geometric solids called crystals. A crystal's shape depends on the way the atoms and molecules join inside it.

Cubic crystal

Triclinic crystal

Orthorhombic crystal

Tetragonal crystal

Monoclinic crystal

Hexagonal crystal

Lightning can make shapes in sand. When it strikes sand, pieces of natural glass, called fulgurites, may be formed. The intense heat vaporizes and melts the sand, fusing it into hollow, branch-like shapes which follow the path taken by the lightning.

A solid lightning bolt?

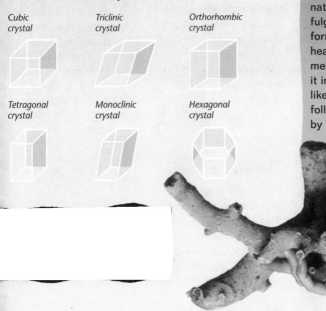

Precious Stones

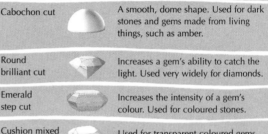

Gemstones are celebrities of the mineral world because they are so rare and beautiful. Of the hundred or so types that exist, diamonds, emeralds, rubies and sapphires are the most precious.

The Star of Africa

This is the world's largest transparent cut diamond. There are larger coloured diamonds, but clear ones are worth more. This pear-shaped jewel was cut from the largest clear diamond ever found: the 3,106 carat* South African Cullinan diamond.

The Star of Africa is in the British royal sceptre. In real life, it's twice as big as this.

Gemstone cuts

Like getting a haircut in a style that suits you, gemstones are cut in a way to enhance their beauty.

Cut		Information
Cabochon cut		A smooth, dome shape. Used for dark stones and gems made from living things, such as amber.
Round brilliant cut		Increases a gem's ability to catch the light. Used very widely for diamonds.
Emerald step cut		Increases the intensity of a gem's colour. Used for coloured stones.
Cushion mixed cut		Used for transparent coloured gems, such as rubies and sapphires.
Marquise fancy cut		Makes a small gem appear larger

The Hope Diamond

Legend has it that this large, deep blue diamond was stolen from an Indian temple hundreds of years ago and brings bad luck. It once belonged to Louis XIV of France and, later, to the English Hope family.

Louis XIV

Diamond, the hardest mineral, is made of carbon, the same element that makes up graphite – the crumbly, black stuff in pencil leads. Diamonds form much deeper in the Earth than graphite, so the greater pressure squeezes them into a stronger structure.

Diamond and pencil lead... the same basic stuff

The Star of India

One of the largest sapphires is called the Star of India. It is deep blue with a star pattern inside and was found hundreds of years ago in Sri Lanka.

*When measuring diamonds, 5 carats = 1 gram.

Diamond geysers

Diamonds form deep down. They are only found near the surface if they were forced up millions of years ago with magma from the mantle, through a rare and violent type of volcano. The cooling magma formed pipe-shaped masses of rock.

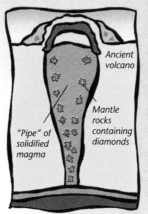

Ancient volcano

Mantle rocks containing diamonds

"Pipe" of solidified magma

Jade – a precious green or white stone – is as tough as steel. It was highly prized in ancient China, and was used to make axes, knives and other weapons.

Not just a pretty sword – jade blades were strong and sharp.

INTERNET LINKS
To find links to websites about jewels and gemstones, go to **www.usborne-quicklinks.com**

Birthstones

Month	Gemstone	Colour	Symbolizes	Mineral	Best gems found
January	Garnet		Loyalty	Hard silicate	Brazil; Russia
February	Amethyst		Sincerity	Quartz	Zambia; Uruguay
March	Aquamarine		Courage	Beryl	Brazil
April	Diamond		Innocence	Pure carbon	South Africa
May	Emerald		Love	Beryl	Colombia
June	Pearl		Health	Calcium carbonate	Persian Gulf
July	Ruby		Contentment	Corundum	Burma
August	Peridot		Happy marriage	Olivine	Arizona; Pakistan
September	Sapphire		Clear thinking	Corundum	Sri Lanka; Burma
October	Opal		Hope	Silica with water	Australia
November	Topaz		Faithfulness	Silicate	Brazil
December	Turquoise		Prosperity	Copper silicate	Iran

Earthquakes

There are about a million earthquakes a year. They are caused by the shifting of the Earth's plates. Most are so tiny that they only show up on special measuring devices, called seismographs. Big quakes occur about every two weeks, but most of these happen under the sea.

A seismograph records earthquake vibrations as lines on paper.

Pacific earthquake zone

Pacific Ocean

Ring of Fire

Ring of Fire

The most earthquake-prone place in the world is an area circling the Pacific Ocean, called the Ring of Fire. Nine out of ten quakes happen there.

INTERNET LINKS
To find links to ground-breaking websites about earthquakes, go to
www.usborne-quicklinks.com

Some animals act strangely when they sense an earthquake coming. In 1975, the people of Haicheng, China, noticed snakes waking early from hibernation. Thousands fled, escaping a huge earthquake, partly thanks to these animal warnings.

Rating rumbles

The power of an earthquake is measured on the Richter scale. Each whole value has 33 times the energy of the one below. Earthquake intensity is measured on the Mercalli scale, which rates effects.

Mercalli	Richter	Effects
1	0.1-2.9	Detectable only by seismometers
2	3.0-3.4	Noticed by a few people on upper floors
3	3.5-4.0	Like a light truck going by. Hanging lights swing.
4	4.1-4.4	Like a heavy truck going by. Windows rattle.
5	4.5-4.8	Sleepers wake up. Small items move. Drinks spill.
6	4.9-5.4	Many people run outside. Heavy furniture moves.
7	5.5-6.0	Walls crack. Loose bricks fall. Hard to stand up.
8	6.1-6.5	Chimneys and weak buildings collapse.
9	6.6-7.0	Well-built houses collapse. Ground cracks.
10	7.1-7.3	Landslides. Many stone buildings collapse.
11	7.4-8.1	Most buildings destroyed. Large cracks in ground.
12	8.2+	Ground moves in waves. Total destruction.

Ten minute terror

Earthquakes usually last less than a minute. The terrible earthquake that destroyed Lisbon, Portugal, in 1755 lasted for a whole ten minutes.

The shockwaves of the 1755 Lisbon earthquake were felt as far as North Africa and Scotland.

Recent major earthquakes	Richter	Deaths	Notes
2003, Boumerdes, Algeria	6.9	2,200	Widespread damage; tsunami waves
2001, Gujarat, India	8.0	20,085	Second strongest quake in Indian history
1995, Kobe, Japan	6.8	6,400	Thousands of buildings destroyed
1990, Manjil-Rudbar, Iran	7.7	50,000	Landslides; cities destroyed
1985, Mexico City, Mexico	8.1	20,000	Thousands of buildings destroyed
1976, Tangshan, China	7.9	655,237	Deadliest 20th century quake
1970, Coast of Peru	7.8	18,000	Town of Yungay buried in rockslide
1964, Prince William Sound, Alaska	8.6	125	Strongest quake in USA's history
1960, Concepcion, Chile	8.7	2,000	Strongest quake ever recorded
1935, Quetta, Pakistan	7.5	30-60,000	Most of city of Quetta destroyed
1923, Tokyo-Kanto, Japan	8.3	142,807	Caused the Great Tokyo Fire
1920, Ningxia-Kansu, China	8.6	200,000	Huge cracks in ground; landslides
1908, Messina, Italy	7.5	70-100,000	Tsunami killed many
1906, San Francisco	7.9	3,000	Deadliest in USA's history; Great Fire

China crisis

China has the worst record for earthquake deaths. In 1556, an earthquake in Shanxi province killed 830,000 people – the deadliest earthquake ever.

Buildings damaged in the terrible Tangshan earthquake of 1976

In the worst earthquakes, the ground rolls in huge waves of destruction. The 1964 Alaskan earthquake lasted seven minutes and cracks opened in the ground up to 90cm wide and 12m deep. One school was split in two.

A car lies crushed under the third floor of an apartment building after an earthquake in San Francisco in 1989.

Volcanoes

There are over 600 active volcanoes on Earth. About half of these are on the Ring of Fire*. Many islands, such as Iceland, are volcanic. Iceland has about 200 volcanoes.

Living dangerously

Ash from volcanoes can make the soil rich. But ash and lava from big eruptions can ruin land for years. Farmers have to hope for the best.

Living by a volcano can be risky.

Eruptions

About 20-30 volcanoes erupt each year. A few erupt almost all the time – Stromboli in Italy goes off every 20 minutes.

Stromboli – little and often

Some volcanoes are dormant (asleep), and can go for years without erupting. In 1902, Mount Pelée, on the island of Martinique, erupted after 50 years of being dormant, killing 29,000 people.

Beware of sleeping volcanoes.

A giant volcanic crater lies buried under Yellowstone Park, USA. It formed 600,000 years ago, in an eruption so huge that it covered most of North America in ash.

Castle Geyser in Yellowstone Park, USA, is powered by a giant underground volcano.

Volcano	Location	Last major eruption	Largest eruption	Facts
Kilauea	Hawaii, USA	continual	1983–now	Most active volcano on Earth
Mt Erebus	Ross Island, Antarctica	continual	1841	Southernmost active volcano
Mt Etna	Sicily, Italy	1992	1669	Europe's highest (3,236m) and liveliest
Nevado del Ruiz	Colombia	1985	1595	Deadliest recent eruption: 24,000 killed
Mauna Loa	Hawaii, USA	1984	1950	Largest active volcano (5,271km²)
Mt St Helens	Washington, USA	1980	2000BC	Largest eruption in US history (1980)
Vesuvius	Naples, Italy	1944	AD79	Eruption in AD79 destroyed Pompeii
Ojos del Salado	Chile/Argentina	unknown	unknown	Highest active volcano (6,887m)
Krakatau	Sumatra, Indonesia	1883	1883	Made loudest sound ever recorded
Mt Tambora	Sumbawa, Indonesia	1815	1815	Largest eruption in history
Mt Fuji	Honshu, Japan	1708	930BC	Highest mountain (3,776m) in Japan

Baby boomer

In a Mexican cornfield in 1943, the volcano Paricutín was born. It began as a 45m crack, spitting ash and scaring farmhands.

A crack in the Earth became a volcano.

Within a few months, its lava flows were 15m deep. In a year, it had a cone higher than the Eiffel Tower in France. In 1952, after nine years of destroying villages and crops, Paricutín's life came to an end.

Rivers of fire

Lava is hot magma (molten rock) flowing above the Earth's surface. There are two types of lava flow. They have Hawaiian names, because much volcano study is done in Hawaii.

aa *(say "ah-ah")*
Stodgy, slow-flowing lava with a rough, broken surface. Forms cone-shaped "stratovolcanoes" from violent eruptions.

pahoehoe
(say "pa-hoy-hoy")
Runny, fizzy lava with a thin skin, often with rope-like wrinkles. Forms dome volcanoes from gentle eruptions.

Mount Etna in Sicily has the strange habit of blowing rings of steam. They measure 200m across, last up to ten minutes, and may rise 1km into the air.

I'm forever blowing steam rings...

As lava from Kilauea, in Hawaii, flows into the Pacific Ocean, it cools to form new land.

INTERNET LINKS

To see a volcano through a live webcam, and much more, go to **www.usborne-quicklinks.com**

Mountains

Around a quarter of Earth's land is covered with mountains that rise 900m or more above sea level. Tibet, in China, is the highest country, averaging 4,572m.

Mountain roots

Just as ships float in water, so also Earth's rocky plates "float" on the denser layer below. As mountains grow, their weight presses the crust down into the mantle, forming roots that act like foundations.

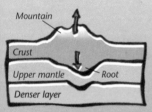

Mountains have roots that push down into the Earth's mantle.

Mountain pile-up

Where continental plates smash together, mountains are built. Ten million years ago, India crashed into Asia. The Asian plate slowly buckled upwards, forming the Himalayas – the highest mountains in the world.

Himalayas
India

The Himalayas are still growing as India pushes into Asia

Mountain ranges	Location	Million years old
Highlands	Scotland	400
Appalachians	USA	250
Urals	Russia	250
Andes	South America	80
Rockies	North America	70
Himalayas	Asia	40
Alps	Europe	15

Old as the hills

All mountain ranges are millions of years old but the tallest ranges, such as the Himalayas, are often younger than the shorter ones. They haven't had so much time to get worn down.

The Himalayas are new kids on the block.

Huge footprints have been found in the Himalayas that don't match any known animal. Many people believe that they are made by giant, ape-like creatures called yetis.

Were these footprints made by man or beast?

Continent	Highest mountain	Height	Location
Asia	Mount Everest	8,850m	Nepal/China
South America	Mount Aconcagua	6,959m	Argentina
North America	Mount McKinley	6,194m	USA
Africa	Mount Kilimanjaro	5,895m	Tanzania
Europe	Mount Elbrus	5,642m	Russia
Antarctica	Vinson Massif	4,897m	Ellsworth Land
Oceania	Mount Wilhelm	4,509m	Papua New Guinea

INTERNET LINKS
To find links to websites about mountains, go to
www.usborne-quicklinks.com

City high

The world's highest capital city is La Paz in Bolivia. It is 3,632m up in the Andes. That's more than a third as high as Mount Everest.

La Paz in Bolivia is known as "the city that touches the sky".

Rocky Mountain goats can climb cliffs that are nearly vertical. Tough pads on their hoofs act as suction cups, stopping them from slipping.

Rocky Mountain goats have sharp hoofs that dig into rock and ice.

Each half of the hoof can move separately for better grip.

Big hearted

Some people live very high up, where there is less oxygen in the air. The Quechua Indians live 4,000m up in the Andes. Mountain people and animals have big hearts and lungs to carry more blood, and so more oxygen.

High life

Different plants and animals are found at different heights up a mountain. Here are some of the highlights of Himalayan life:

8,000m

Alpine chough

Cushion pinks

Snow leopard

5,000m

Blue poppy

Tibetans take their yaks as high as 4,600m to graze in the summer.

3,000m

Red panda

Tibetans have terraced the lower slopes to grow their crops.

1,000m

Longest mountain ranges	Location	Length
Andes	South America	7,240km
Rocky Mountains	North America	6,030km
Himalaya/Karakoram/Hindu Kush	Asia	3,860km
Great Dividing Range	Australia	3,620km
Transantarctic Mountains	Antarctica	3,540km

Caves and Caverns

Caves prove that water can be stronger than rock. Water flowing underground slowly eats away at rocks until they collapse, forming caves and caverns (which are just large caves).

In Mexico, there are some deep caves with walls that drip burning acid. In spite of this, tiny, living things called bacteria live here. They mix with minerals to form dangling strands of acid slime known as "snottites".

These slimy formations are called snottites – remind you of anything?

Cave critters

Cave animals are adapted to their cold, dark homes. Because it is so dark, some are blind and use other senses to find their way around. Many don't have skin colour to protect them from the Sun's rays.

Name		Adaptations to cave life
Little brown bat		Find their way by bouncing echoes off objects ("echo location")
Olm (cave salamander)		Blind; pale skin; sharp sense of smell; can go without food for long periods
Northern cavefish		Blind; pale skin; vibration sensors on head; carry young in gills
Cave cricket		Very long legs to clamber over rocks; colour camouflages against limestone

To the Batcave!

Bracken Cave in Texas, USA, houses the world's largest bat colony. Up to 20 million Mexican free-tailed bats call it home.

The bats of Bracken Cave can eat 250 tonnes of insects in a night.

Water sculptures

Water that drips through and over cavern rock contains dissolved minerals. These minerals can slowly build up into strange and beautiful shapes. Cavers have given names to some of these shapes:

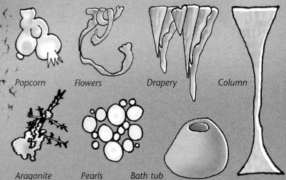

Popcorn   *Flowers*   *Drapery*   *Column*

Aragonite   *Pearls*   *Bath tub*

Underground wonders	Country	Record
Mammoth Cave	USA	Longest cave system (563km)
Voronja Cave	Georgia	Deepest cave (1.7km)
Sarawak Chamber	Malaysia	Largest cavern (700m long; 300m wide; 70m high)
Sistema Chac-Mol	Mexico	Longest stalactite (12m)
Cueva San Martin Infierno	Cuba	Tallest stalagmite (67.2m)
Tham Sao Hin	Thailand	Tallest column (61.5m)
Ruby Falls	USA	Highest undergound waterfall (44m)
Son Trach river	Vietnam	Longest underground river (11.3km)
Kazumura Cave	USA	Longest lava tube (65.5km)
Painted Cave	USA	Longest sea cave (374m)

Stalacites grow down from the roof.

Stalagmites grow up from the floor.

Cave art

In 1940, two adventurous boys discovered some caves in Lascaux, France. On the cave walls, they were amazed to find beautiful paintings of horses, bison and other animals, painted 17,000 years ago.

Stone-age graffiti?

INTERNET LINKS
To find links to amazing websites about caves and caverns, go to
www.usborne-quicklinks.com

The world's tallest underground room is in Baiyu Dong cave, China. It is 424m high.

Can you imagine a room as tall as New York's Empire State Building?

Crystal caverns

Deep in the Naica mines in Mexico are the world's largest known crystals. These are giant gypsum crystals that have formed in the hot, sauna-like atmosphere of a single cavern. Some, measuring 15m high, are as tall as pine trees.

The Cave of the Giants lives up to name.

Tundra

About a tenth of Earth's land is covered by a huge, frozen area called the tundra. It stretches between the Arctic ice and the Northern forests.

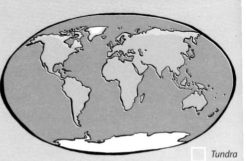

Tundra

Permanent frost

The frozen layer of soil beneath the tundra never thaws, and is called the permafrost. In parts of Siberia it can be as deep as 1.5km.

Tundra

Permafrost

The permafrost stops water draining away, so in summer the tundra is riddled with bogs and ponds.

Deep freeze

The permafrost can act like a deep freeze. Well-preserved remains of Ice Age mammoths have been found in Siberia and Alaska – even whole bodies.

Over 50 deep-frozen mammoths have been found in the permafrost.

Tundra statistics

Area	13,000,000km²
Permafrost depth (average)	305-610m
Winter temperature	-29 to -33°C
Summer temperature	3 to 12°C

Shaggy goat story

Musk oxen may look like bison but they are actually related to goats and are very nimble for their size. They live all year in the tundra. Their shaggy hair grows down nearly to their hoofs, keeping them warm.

Only humans can grow longer hair than musk oxen.

Tundra people

People have lived in the tundra for thousands of years. Here are some native tundra people.

People	Where they live	Population
Sakha	Russia	400,000
Komi	Russia	344,500
Inuit	Russia, Alaska, Greenland, Canada	130,000
Sami	Russia, Sweden, Finland, Norway	100,000
Eskimo	Alaska, Russia	48,500
Indian tribes	Alaska	36,500
Nenet	Russia	34,500
Even	Russia	17,000
Chukchi	Russia	15,000

Winter white

As winter approaches, many tundra animals turn white to blend in with the snow. In spring, they change back. Here are some animals in their winter colours.

Ptarmigan

Snowshoe rabbit

Snowy owl

Stoat

Arctic fox

In winter, the north-east Siberian tundra under its layer of snow and ice becomes even colder than the North Pole.

Oil highway

The Trans-Alaskan oil pipeline stretches 1,300km from the Arctic Ocean to southern Alaska. It has to be heated to at least 45°C to stop the oil freezing inside the pipe.

The pipeline is raised in places to let large animals get under.

Watch your step in the tundra – you could be walking on top of a forest. Near the treeline, the trees are so blasted by the wind that they cling to the ground.

Ground willow can be 5m long but only 10cm high.

Red hot

Many tundra plants have striking, dark red leaves. This helps them to soak up as much of the Sun's life-giving heat as they can in the cold climate.

Red bearberry leaves

INTERNET LINKS
To find links to websites about the tundra, go to **www.usborne-quicklinks.com**

Commuter caribou

Huge herds of up to 100,000 caribou (North American reindeer) trek 600km north to the tundra each spring to give birth. They return south every autumn. Caribou have been following the same routes for hundreds of years.

Following the leader – a line of caribou may stretch for 300km.

Northern Forests

The largest forest area in the world is called the taiga (say "tie-ga"). It stretches from Alaska to Canada, and from Scandinavia to Siberia.

Taiga

Deciduous forest

Most of the trees in the taiga are conifers. These have needles rather than broad leaves, and are mostly evergreen. Their seeds are protected in woody cones.

Further south (see map), the forests are broad-leaved and deciduous. This means that the trees lose their leaves in autumn.

Conifers

Red cedar

Cypress

Hemlock

Larch

Spruce

Juniper

Silver fir

Douglas fir

Yew

Pine

Redwood

Part of conifer	Used for
Timber	Furniture, matches, tannic acid (used in making leather goods)
Pulp	Paper, plastics, Rayon
Cellulose	Cellophane, turpentine
Needles	Pine oil (used in soap), vitamins A and E

King cone

The longest pine cones come from sugar pines in the USA. They grow 66cm long – nearly two-thirds the length of a baseball bat.

Sugar pine cone

Nearly three-quarters of the world's timber and almost all of the world's paper comes from conifers. Paper is made from leftover timber cuttings and thin trees. From one tree, you could make 800 copies of this book.

INTERNET LINKS
To find links to tremendous websites about trees, go to **www.usborne-quicklinks.com**

All change

The most amazing thing about deciduous trees is the way their leaves change colour before they fall in autumn. This is because their leaves lose a green chemical called chlorophyll as they die. With the green colour gone, other colours in the leaf are revealed.

Autumn leaves go out in a blaze of colour.

Each person in the USA uses enough wooden items a year to make a tree 30m tall and 41cm wide. That's over 280 million trees a year. Using recycled paper saves trees.

Many recycled products show this symbol.

Broad-leaved deciduous trees

Ash

Alder

Oak

Birch

Beech

Maple

Elm

Chestnut

Record-breaking trees

Giant sequoia, California, USA	Largest tree ("General Sherman") 31m around trunk; 83.8m tall
Montezuma cypress, Oaxaca, Mexico	Broadest tree ("El Tule") 36m around trunk
Aspen grove, Utah, USA	A grove of quaking aspen ("Pando"), which is joined at the roots, making it the largest living thing, at 0.81km² in area.
Coast redwood, California, USA	Tallest tree (the "Mendocino tree") 112m
Bristlecone pine, California, USA	Oldest tree ("Methuselah") 4,767 years

Fireproof trees

Trees with thick bark, such as pine and sequoia, can survive fierce forest fires. These tough trees are only scarred by the fire and their wood is unharmed. Some forest fires spread at 15kph and the roar they make can be heard 1.6km away.

Coast redwoods, a type of sequoia, are the tallest trees in the world. They can grow to over five times the height of a house.

Tropical Rainforests

Rainforests stretch around the middle of the Earth like a green belt. These ancient forests have broad-leaved evergreen trees that are home to Earth's most amazing variety of animals.

Tropical rainforests are hot and wet. At least 250cm of rain falls there each year.

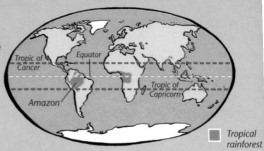

Tropical rainforest

INTERNET LINKS
To find links to websites about the world's rainforests, go to **www.usborne-quicklinks.com**

Jeepers creepers

Lianas are giant, woody vines that climb trees and hang down from the rainforest canopy. The longest are over 1km.

Lianas are strong enough for monkeys (and Tarzan) to swing on.

! The rainforest could vanish by 2030 unless its destruction is slowed down. Since 1800, half of it has been cut down for fuel, timber, and to make farmland, or has been lost through fire and drought.

Rainforest layers

Emergent layer
Huge trees mushroom through the layer below, searching for sunlight. Some are as tall as a twelve-floor building.

Canopy
Broad treetops make a forest roof, tied together with vines. The canopy is so thick, rain can take ten minutes to reach the forest floor. Most rainforest animals live in this layer.

Understorey
Shady, open area with young trees. Many insects live here.

Forest floor
Leaf litter is quickly eaten by insects.

Amazon forest being burned down to make farmland

Air plants

Air plants take in all the food and moisture they need from the air. They grow on trees high in the canopy. Some have leaves which cup water, helping them to survive dry spells.

Tadpoles in trees? Tree frogs lay their eggs in air-plant pools.

The rainforest may only cover 6% of the Earth's land, but over 50% of all plant and animal species live there. One rainforest in Peru houses more types of bird than the whole of the USA.

Quetzals live in South American rainforests.

Ferns and mosses grow well in the warm, damp rainforest.

Healing herbs

Many medicines are made from rainforest plants. Quinine, the cure for malaria, comes from the cinchona tree. Over 70% of chemicals used to fight cancer come from the rainforest.

Rosy periwinkle – not just a pretty flower. It contains a chemical that fights cancer.

Rainforest record breakers

Smallest bird Bee hummingbird – 5.6cm long

Smallest deer Mouse deer – 50cm long, 25cm high

Largest rodent Capybara – 1m long, 60cm high

Largest frog Goliath frog – 40cm long

Largest snail African land snail – 25cm long

Largest spider Goliath birdeater – 25cm wide

Largest scorpion Emperor scorpion – 15cm long

Biggest butterfly Queen Alexandra's birdwing – 30cm wide

Largest centipede Peruvian giant centipede – 28cm long

Butterfly giant – Queen Alexandra's birdwing

Big stinkers

At 1m wide, the rafflesia is the world's biggest flower. It's amazing to see but not so great to sniff, as it smells of rotting meat. The smell attracts insects that spread the flower's pollen around the forest.

Rafflesia – stinking out the Malaysian rainforest.

Rainforest crops

Materials	Gum, rubber
Timber	Mahogany, teak
Fruit	Bananas, pineapples
Spices	Paprika, pepper
Oils	Palm, patchouli
Fibres	Jute, rattan
Beans	Cocoa, coffee

Grasslands and Savannahs

About a quarter of the Earth's land is covered by huge expanses of grassy land called grasslands and savannahs. There is enough rain to stop this land turning to desert, but not enough for forests to grow.

Only patches of grass, scrub, bushes and a few trees grow on savannahs.

Grasslands have more grass and can be used for growing crops, such as wheat, or as pasture for grazing animals. Some grasses grow very tall.

Elephant grass grows up to 4.5m high in the savannah.

Steppes
Prairie
Llanos
Savannah
Pampas
Campos
Veldt
Scrub

Grasslands and savannahs are known by different names in different regions.

Grassland	Name
Argentina	Pampas
North America	Prairie
South Africa	Veldt
Central Asia	Steppes
Australia	Scrub
Savannah	**Name**
East Africa	Savannah
Brazil	Campos
Venezuela	Llanos

Saiga antelope have inflatable noses. Their noses filter out dust in the dry summer months, and warm up cold air in winter.

This saiga antelope can blow its nose.

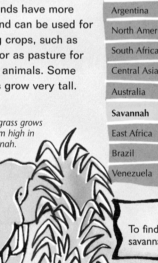

INTERNET LINKS
To find links to websites about grasslands and savannahs, go to **www.usborne-quicklinks.com**

Upside-down trees

African baobab trees have enormous, swollen trunks which store water for the dry season. Their branches are stumpy and look more like roots. Some old, hollow baobab trees have even been used as bus shelters or houses.

Baobab tree

Serious cereal

Cereal crops are wild grasses that have been cultivated by people. They are our main source of food. The pictures show the main crops and the number of tonnes harvested worldwide in 2002, starting with sugar cane, the biggest crop.

Sugar cane
1,287,804,970

Maize
602,026,822

Rice
579,476,722

Wheat
568,108,477

Barley
131,558,348

Sorghum
55,340,825

Oats
27,711,619

Millet
25,762,606

Rye
20,747,085

All the rice produced in the world in one day would make a pile the size of the Great Pyramid in Egypt.

Rice is the main food for over half the world. Over 90% of rice is grown in Asia.

Wind power

Grasses have flowers, but are not brightly coloured because they don't need to attract pollen-carrying insects. Wind carries their pollen from flower to flower.

There about 10,000 types of grass.

Now you see me

The colours of savannah predators help them to stalk their prey unseen. Striped or spotted animals, such as leopards and cheetahs, are hard to see from a distance. A lion's tawny colour hides it in the long, dry grass.

Grass gourmets

Grazing animals are very choosy about which part of a plant they eat. The same piece of grass may provide lunch for several different grazers.

Watch out, there's a lion lying in wait in this long grass.

Zebras nibble the tips, wildebeest munch the middle, and gazelle gobble the rest.

Deserts

One-fifth of the Earth's land is covered by desert. Only 15% of deserts are made up of sand, though. The rest are bare rock or have gravelly and pebbly surfaces. All deserts get less than 25cm of rainfall a year, so very little can grow there.

Desert areas

Great Sahara

The Sahara is the largest desert on Earth. It is about the size of the USA and covers over a third of Africa. Millions of years ago, it wasn't desert, but was covered in forests and grasslands teeming with wildlife.

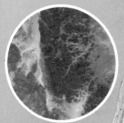

Aerial view of ancient riverbeds branching through the Sahara

Deserts of the world

Hot deserts are hot by day, all year round. Cold deserts have hot summers and cooler winters.

Desert	Location	Area (km²)	Type
Sahara	North Africa	9,100,000	Hot
Arabian	Saudi Arabia	2,300,000	Hot
Gobi	Mongolia/China	1,295,000	Cold
Patagonian	Argentina	673,000	Cold
Kalahari	Botswana	520,000	Hot
Taklimakan	Western China	349,400	Cold
Great Victoria	Western/South Australia	348,750	Hot
Great Sandy	Western Australia	267,250	Hot
Great Basin	USA	190,000	Cold
Atacama	Chile	140,000	Cold
Namib	Namibia	135,000	Cold

Colossal cacti

Cacti are only found in American deserts. The tallest is the 19m cardón cactus of the Sonoran Desert, Mexico. It lives for hundreds of years.

Up to 90% of a cactus is water it stores for dry spells.

The Atacama Desert in Chile is the driest place on Earth. Parts of it had no rain for 400 years, from 1570 to 1971. In other parts it has never rained.

Atacama – as dry as it gets

Worn away

Desert winds can be tough on rocks. Soft rock is blasted away by sand carried on the wind. This is called erosion. Harder rock is left behind, sometimes revealing spectacular rock shapes.

This huge, balancing boulder was carved out by desert winds.

INTERNET LINKS
To find links to websites about deserts and desert life, go to **www.usborne-quicklinks.com**

Desert animal	Lives in	Survival skills
Fennec fox	Sahara	Large ears help it lose heat.
Jerboa	Sahara	Long hind legs help it jump away from predators.
Sidewinder (a snake)	USA	Lifts and loops its body sideways to reduce contact with the hot sand.
Arabian camel (dromedary)	Arabian desert	Hump stores fat, and can store water in its stomach for days.
Thorny devil (a lizard)	Australia	Grooves on its back collect and channel dew into its mouth.
Tadpole shrimp	Deserts worldwide	Eggs lie dried in sand for years, only hatching if rain comes.

When a Texas horned lizard wants to hide itself against the desert soil, it can make itself lighter or darker. If predators attack, it has one more trick – it squirts blood from its eyes.

Creeping dunes

Some sand dunes move. Wind blowing up one side blows sand down the other. Dunes creep forward 10-50m a year, sometimes covering villages and oases.

The Sossusvlei dunes in the Namib Desert are some of the world's highest – up to 300m.

Mirages

Hot deserts are famous for mirages: tricks of the light that make pools of water seem to appear, then vanish as you get closer to them. You might see the same effect on roads on hot days.

How mirages work

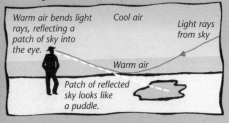

Warm air bends light rays, reflecting a patch of sky into the eye.

Cool air

Light rays from sky

Warm air

Patch of reflected sky looks like a puddle.

An inviting pool in the desert? No – it's a mirage.

Lakes and Rivers

Only 3% of Earth's water is fresh – the rest is salty. Two-thirds of fresh water is frozen in ice sheets and glaciers. Most of the little that remains is in lakes, rivers and under the ground.

Continent	Longest river	Length
Africa	Nile	6,671km
South America	Amazon	6,440km
Asia	Chang Jiang (Yangtze)	6,380km
North America	Mississippi-Missouri-Red Rock	6,019km
Oceania	Murray-Darling	3,718km
Europe	Volga	3,700km

Deep in Siberia

The world's deepest lake is also the oldest. Lake Baikal in Siberia, Russia, is over 1.6km at its deepest point and contains one-fifth of all the world's fresh water. It is 25 million years old.

The Petronas Towers in Malaysia – the world's tallest buildings – would be lost in Lake Baikal.

! The largest freshwater fish is the wels catfish* (the record is 5m long). These giants were brought to the UK by landowners in the 1800s, thinking they would be good to eat, but they proved hard to catch. Some still lurk in British lakes today, even preying on ducks.

Going nowhere

Not all rivers flow to the sea — some disappear. The Okavango, in Botswana, Africa, fans out into a mass of streams and swampland 15,500km² in area. Its waters finally vanish into the Kalahari Desert.

Largest lakes and inland seas	Location	Area
Caspian Sea	Western Asia	370,999km²
Lake Superior	USA/Canada	82,414km²
Lake Victoria	Tanzania/Uganda	69,215km²
Lake Huron	USA/Canada	59,596km²
Lake Michigan	USA	58,016km²
Lake Tanganyika	Tanzania/Congo	32,764km²
Lake Baikal	Russia	31,500km²

*The Beluga sturgeon is bigger, up to 8m long, but it lives mainly at sea.

Highest waterfalls	Location	Height
Angel Falls	Venezuela	979m
Tugela Falls	South Africa	948m
Kjelsfossen	Norway	840m
Mtarazi	Zimbabwe	762m
Yosemite Falls	USA	739m
Mongefoss	Norway	714m
Espelandsfoss	Norway	703m

INTERNET LINKS

To find links to websites about lakes and rivers, go to www.usborne-quicklinks.com

Amazing Amazon

The river that carries most water is the Amazon. Starting 5,200m up in the Andes, it ends on the Atlantic coast in a maze of islands and channels 300km wide. Its silty, yellow-brown fresh water flows 180km out to sea.

Piranhas are ferocious, flesh-eating fish. Their teeth are so sharp that Amazonian Indians use them as scissors.

Floating islands

Titicaca, 3,810m up in the Peruvian Andes, is the world's highest sailable lake. Floating on it are islands, some as big as football fields, made from matted reeds. Uros Indians make the islands and live on them. They also build their houses and boats from the reeds.

A Uros reed boat on Lake Titicaca

Moving falls

The force of the Niagara Falls slowly grinds away the rocks at its edge, causing the Falls to move. Today, the Falls are midway along the Niagara River, on the Canada-USA border between Lake Ontario and Lake Erie. 10,000 years ago, the Falls were 11km further downstream.

The Falls 10,000 years ago

Niagara Falls today

In 25,000 years, the Falls will vanish as they reach Lake Erie.

The Seashore

If all the world's coastlines were stretched out end to end, they would measure 504,000km – long enough to go around the Earth 13 times.

INTERNET LINKS
To find links to websites about the seashore, go to **www.usborne-quicklinks.com**

Highest sea cliffs

North America	
Molokai, Hawaii	1,010m
South America	
Coastal Range, N. Chile	1,000m
Asia	
Chingshui Cliffs, Taiwan	760m
Europe	
Enniberg, Faroe Islands	754m
Oceania	
Port Arthur, Tasmania	300m
Africa	
Cape Point, South Africa	249m

Changing coast

The coastline can change position over a long period of time. Many ancient Roman ports around the Mediterranean Sea, such as Caesarea on the coast of Israel, are now underwater. By contrast, on England's south coast, the old port of Rye, in Sussex, is now 3km inland.

Rye 250 years ago

Rye today

Rising tide

The sea rises and falls on the shore twice a day, at high and low tides. The biggest difference in tides is in the Bay of Fundy, Canada, where high tide reaches 16m.

Stormy weather

In winter, waves crash onto the northern shores of the Pacific Ocean with the same force as a car hitting a wall at 145kph. Storm waves on the west coast of North America once tossed a rock weighing 61kg, the weight of a grown person, 28m up onto the roof of a lighthouse.

Portland Head in Maine, USA, is made of tough rock that has resisted storms for hundreds of years.

Wearing and grinding

Sand is made from rock that is worn down as it is washed out to sea by rivers, or ground down by waves battering cliffs. Some beaches have sand of one colour, such as the black lava stone beaches of Tahiti. Others are a mixture of colours, made from various rocks, worn-down coral, or seashells.

Sand colour	Made from
Black	Lava stone
Grey	Granite, feldspar
Tan	Granite, quartz
Yellow	Quartz
Gold	Mica
Red	Garnet
Pink	Feldspar
White	Coral, seashells, quartz
Green	Olivine

The coast at Martha's Vineyard, in Massachusets, USA, is worn away so quickly by waves – 1.7m each year – that a lighthouse standing there has had to be moved inland three times.

Here we go again...

Towering dunes

Some sand dunes on France's Atlantic coast reach an amazing 108m high – seven times higher than most beach dunes. The dunes, blown by wind, creep slowly inland by about 6m a year. They may bury buildings and even whole forests.

The enormous Dune of Pilat at Arcachon on France's west coast

Rock carving

Coastlines are always changing. On rocky shores, waves pound against the cliffs, flinging up boulders, pebbles and sand. These grind away the rock, forming headlands, caves, arches and stacks.

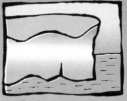

Headland

Sea cave

Arch

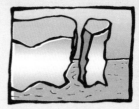

Stack

41

The Ocean

Two-thirds of Earth's surface is covered by salt water. It is divided into five oceans but they are all connected. The largest ocean is the Pacific. At its widest point (between Panama and Malaysia) it stretches for 17,700km – nearly halfway around the world.

Earth's oceans	Area
Pacific Ocean	155,557,000km²
Atlantic Ocean	76,762,000km²
Indian Ocean	68,556,000km²
Southern Ocean	20,327,000km²
Arctic Ocean	14,056,000km²

1 Pacific Ocean
2 Atlantic Ocean
3 Indian Ocean
4 Southern Ocean
5 Arctic Ocean

Most whale sounds are too low for us to hear.

Oceans and seas

Parts of the Earth's five oceans are divided into areas called seas.

Largest seas	Area	Ocean
Weddell Sea	8,000,000km²	Southern
Arabian Sea	7,456,000km²	Indian
South China Sea	2,974,000km²	Pacific
Mediterranean Sea	2,505,000km²	Atlantic
Barents Sea	1,300,000km²	Arctic

Whalesongs

Sound travels through water over four times as quickly as it does through air. Low-pitched whalesongs can carry for hundreds of kilometres under the sea. Whales may sing to attract a distant mate.

Cucumber city

Thousands of sea cucumbers – simple animals related to sea urchins – live deep in trenches in the seabed. If you weighed all the animals that live on the seabed, about 95% of their combined weight would be made up of sea cucumbers.

Sea cucumber – animal not vegetable

The surface of the Moon has been much more thoroughly explored than the deep oceans of our own planet.

We call the dark patches on the Moon seas and oceans, but they are as dry as dust.

What has eight arms, eyes the size of dinner plates and grows longer than a double-decker bus? Answer: a giant squid. Although they are some of the largest creatures in the ocean, scientists have yet to study a live adult.

Would you like to wrestle with an animal whose eyes were bigger than your head?

Deeply fishy

Most plants and animals only live at particular depths of the ocean. Many fish are coloured to make them hard to see at their depth.

Surface *Masses of tiny floating plants and animals, called plankton. Fish living here are often blue, green or violet.*

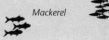

Mackerel   Herring

Squid

100m *Plants don't grow far below 100m, as there is little light.*

Hatchet fish   Tuna

200m *In the "twilight zone", most fish are pale or silvery*

Great white shark   Deep-sea eel   Jellyfish

1000m *In the dark depths, fish are mostly black, or dark-coloured. Some creatures are bright red, as red light can't reach these depths, making them nearly invisible.*

Lantern fish

Many deep-sea animals have lights on their bodies.   Angler fish

4000m *Over half of the ocean bed lies at 4,000m or deeper.*

Undersea landscape

If the oceans were drained away, an amazing landscape would be revealed. Running through the Atlantic Ocean is the world's longest mountain range: the Mid-Atlantic Ridge. Lying between Japan and New Guinea is the Mariana Trench – a valley that plunges 11km down to the deepest point on Earth.

INTERNET LINKS
To find links to websites about seas and oceans, and ocean life, go to
www.usborne-quicklinks.com

A 3-D map of part of the Mid-Atlantic Ridge

43

Poles Apart

The North Pole is in the middle of the huge Arctic ice cap, which floats on the Arctic Ocean. There is no land there.

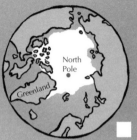

The Arctic □ *Ice cap*

Arctic facts

Area of ice	10,000,000km² (permanent) 14,090,000km² (winter)
Ice cap thickness	Up to 1.5km
Sea ice thickness	3m (average)
Arctic Ocean depth	1,300m (average); 5,450m (greatest)
Area of Greenland ice sheet	1,479,000km²
Thickness of Greenland ice	1.6–3km
Temperature at North Pole	-32°C (average)
North Pole first reached by	Robert Peary and Matthew Henson (USA), 1909
Nearest Settlement to Pole	Siorapaluk, Greenland
Examples of wildlife	Polar bear, snowy owl, Arctic fox, walrus, common seal, hooded seal

"Green" land

Greenland – Earth's largest island – is not very green. 85% of it is covered in ice. It was named by an early settler, Eric the Red, who was trying to persuade fellow Vikings to come and join him.

In 1958, the first nuclear submarine, *USS Nautilus*, became the first vessel to travel directly under the North Pole.

USS Nautilus in New York

Flooded cities

The polar ice sheets hold over 2% of Earth's water. If they melted, the sea level would rise by over 60m. Many coastal areas and major cities would be drowned.

Europe if the ice sheets melted

□ *Underwater* ■ *Dry land*

Hunt the seal

Arctic seals need to come up for air every 20 minutes. When the seas are frozen, the seals chew big breathing holes in the ice.

Polar bears hunt seals, waiting patiently by the breathing holes. When a seal comes up for air, the bear grabs it.

An Arctic seal takes its last breath.

INTERNET LINKS
To find links to websites about the Poles, go to
www.usborne-quicklinks.com

White land

Antarctica is land, but is covered in glaciers that hold 90% of all the ice on Earth.

Antarctica
- ☐ Ice cap
- ☐ Ice shelf

Roald the bold

In 1911, the trailblazing Norwegian explorer, Roald Amundsen, was the first person to reach the South Pole. Fifteen years later, with the Italian Umberto Nobile, he flew on the first airship over the North Pole.

Roald Amundsen

Antarctic facts

Area of ice	4,000,000km² (permanent) 21,000,000km² (winter)
Ice cap thickness	Up to 4km
Sea ice thickness	4m (average)
Southern Ocean depth	4,200m (average); 7,235m (greatest)
Temperature at South Pole	-50°C (average)
South Pole first reached by	Roald Amundsen (Norway), 1911
Nearest settlement to Pole	No permanent Antarctic settlements
Examples of wildlife	Penguin, blue whale, elephant seal, albatross, Weddell seal, leopard seal

Deep water

Lake Vostok is a ma prehistoric lake sea 3.6km beneath th of east Anta coldest pla (-89.2°C). its water is ke heat from in

Antarctica is a desert. Inland, less than 5cm of new snow falls in a year. Most of the snow blowing around there has been lifted and shifted by winds.

The shadowy shape of a lake deep beneath the Antarctic ice

Antarctica, 2,400m above sea level on average, is the highest continent. It is split in two by the Transantarctic Mountains (below), one of the longest mountain ranges in the world.

Glaciers and Icebergs

Glaciers are masses of ice that move slowly down mountains or through valleys. They cover a tenth of Earth's dry surface.

Continent	Longest glacier	Length
Antarctica	Lambert-Fisher glacier	515km
Europe	Novaya Zemlya glacier, Russia	418km
North America	Bering glacier, Alaska	204km
Asia	Biafao-Hispar glacier, Pakistan	125km
South America	Upsala glacier, Andes, Chile	60km
Oceania	Tasman glacier, New Zealand	29km
Africa	Credner glacier, Kilimanjaro, Tanzania	1km

Deep freeze

In 1820, three climbers died when they fell into a crack in a glacier on Mont Blanc in the Alps. Forty-one years later, their bodies emerged, well-preserved, from the glacier's melting snout. Cracks in glaciers are called crevasses and can be 40m deep.

Mind the gap!

Tropical ice

Glaciers are even found near the equator, on mountains over 6,000m high. There is glacier ice 60m deep on Mount Kilimanjaro in Tanzania.

! 75% of all the fresh water on Earth is frozen in glaciers. That's the equivalent of 60 years of non-stop rain.

Birth of a berg

A glacier's melting end is called its snout. Icebergs are made, or "calved", when pieces of glacier break off the

Pacier glacier

Most glaciers creep slowly down mountains, at 3–60cm a day, but the fastest, the Columbia glacier in Alaska, moves up to 35m every day.

Icebergs being calved from Margerie Glacier in Glacier Bay, Alaska, USA

Biggest berg

The largest iceberg ever recorded was 31,000km² in area – that's slightly larger than Belgium. It was seen off the Antarctic coast in 1956.

Belgium

Tallest berg

The tallest iceberg ever seen, off west Greenland, was 167m high – one and a half times as tall as the Eiffel Tower in Paris.

Hidden depths

Only one-tenth of an iceberg shows above the water. If, for example, the iceberg that sank the *Titanic* had shown 30m above the water, then there must have been another 270m below.

The tip of the iceberg is only a fraction of what lies beneath.

One Arctic iceberg drifted 4,000km, nearly as far south as Bermuda. An Antarctic iceberg drifted for 5,500km, nearly as far north as Rio de Janeiro in Brazil.

Big icebergs can drift a very long way before melting.

Iceberg ahoy!

The International Ice Patrol keeps track of icebergs in the North Atlantic, warning ships of any danger. The Patrol was set up after the great liner *RMS Titanic* sank after hitting an iceberg on April 14, 1912. Over 1,500 people drowned.

The biggest icebergs are in Antarctica. Can you spot the penguins?

Iceberg classes	Height above sea level	Length
Growler	under 1m	under 5m
Bergy bit	1-5m	5-15m
Small iceberg	5-15m	16-60m
Medium iceberg	16-45m	61-120m
Large iceberg	46-75m	121-200m
Very large iceberg	over 75m	over 200m

Iceberg shapes

Tabular   Dome   Pinnacle

Blocky   Wedge   Drydock

INTERNET LINKS
To find links to the coolest ice websites, go to **www.usborne-quicklinks.com**

Natural Resources

We use resources from the Earth to give us energy for heat and light. The chart below shows how much of the energy we use comes from natural resources. Renewable resources are those that can be reused or regrown.

Resource	Origin	% World energy	Renewable
Oil	Underground/undersea	34.8%	✗
Coal	Underground	23.5%	✗
Natural gas	Underground	21.1%	✗
Wood and waste	Trees/industry/households	11.0%	✓
Nuclear power	Energy released from atoms	6.8%	✗
Hydropower	Rivers and waterfalls	2.3%	✓
Geothermal	Underground hot water/steam	0.44%	✓
Solar	Energy from sunlight	0.04%	✓
Wind	Wind energy	0.03%	✓
Tidal	Wave energy	0.004%	✓

The Sun gives warmth and light that can be changed into electricity.

Fossil fools?

Fossil fuels (oil, coal and gas) were made from the remains of plants and animals buried beneath the sea millions of years ago. Some day, fossil fuels will run out. At the rate we are using them, we may see oil shortages by 2020, and run low on gas by 2040. Coal may last until 2200.

The remains of prehistoric plants can be seen in these lumps of coal.

INTERNET LINKS
To find links to websites about the world's natural resources, go to **www.usborne-quicklinks.com**

Well, well...

About a third of the world's oil comes from undersea oil wells. A North Sea oil platform can produce 8,000,000 litres of oil a day. That would fill eight Olympic-sized swimming pools.

Under 5% of the world's population live in the USA, but they use more than 25% of the world's oil and electricity.

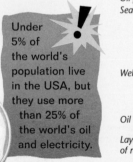

Oil platform —
Seabed —

Well —

Oil reserve —

Layers of rock

48

Sunny side up

The Sun is the biggest energy source we have: in one hour it beams more energy to Earth, in the form of sunlight, than the world uses in a year. The Sun's energy can be collected using solar panels. In places with no mains electricity – parts of Kenya, Africa, for example – many homes power lamps, radios and TVs with solar panels on their roofs.

This house runs on sunshine.

Paraguay in South America generates nearly all its electricity from rivers and waterfalls.

Hydropower

Over a sixth of the world's electricity is generated by the force of water. Electricity generated by water flowing in rivers and over waterfalls is called hydropower.

Country	% of world hydropower
Canada	13.2%
Brazil	11.3%
USA	10.2%
China	8.2%
Russia	6.1%
Norway	5.2%
Japan	3.6%
Sweden	2.9%
India	2.7%
France	2.7%

Staying warm in Iceland

In Iceland, water that's been warmed inside the Earth is used to heat buildings and even open-air swimming pools. It is also piped under the ground to melt snow and ice. In winter, 2,300 litres of naturally boiling water is pumped into the capital city, Reykjavik, every second.

*Water heated by this geothermal** power station in Iceland is used as an open-air swimming pool.*

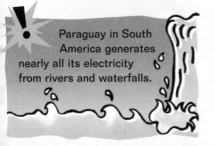

Oil products	Coal products
Petrol (gasoline)	Plastics
Diesel fuel	Heavy chemicals*
Kerosene (jet fuel)	Perfumes
Plastics	Insecticides
Paraffin wax	Antiseptics
Medicines	Road surfaces
Explosives	Coal gas
Pesticides	
Detergents	*Many things we use are made from oil and coal.*
Cosmetics	
Paints	

* Chemicals used in bulk in industry and farming
**Geothermal energy: Earth's natural heat energy

Earth's Problems

Most of the Earth's problems are caused by humans. We are using up fossil fuels and spoiling land, polluting air and water, and even changing the weather along the way.

Global warming

The world is getting warmer. Many scientists think the large amount of carbon dioxide gas made by burning fossil fuels is partly to blame.

Coal-fired power station, UK

Trees soak up carbon dioxide, using it to grow, but the destruction of the rainforest means there are fewer trees to do this.

Problems caused by global warming

- Storms and floods
- Deadly heatwaves
- Droughts and forest fires
- Loss of the northern forests
- Spread of disease-carrying insects
- Shifting seasons confusing wildlife
- Melting glaciers and rising sea-level

Gone forever

Animal species die out naturally over time, but many are now becoming extinct extremely quickly.

Scientists think that by 2030 nearly a quarter of mammal species might have disappeared.

There are only about 7,000 tigers left in the wild.

Mammals in danger	Number in wild	Threats
Amur leopard	55	Hunted for fur; used in traditional medicine
Javan rhino	60	Homes destroyed by logging; hunted for horns
Baiji dolphin	150	Water pollution
Wild bactrian camel	350	Hunted for meat; seen as competition with livestock
Silvery gibbon	400	Homes destroyed by logging and clearing for farmland

There are six billion people on Earth. By 2030, there could be eight billion – a third as many again. There is space on Earth for them all, but sharing food and fuel fairly will be a huge challenge.

Mining

Mining for minerals can spoil massive areas of land and cause pollution. Poisonous waste from mining can wash into rivers, killing wildlife and giving people health problems. Mining is also very dangerous: 40 miners are killed each day, on average.

Water waste

Of the 90 million tonnes of fish taken from the oceans each year, a quarter are thrown back, unwanted. Most of these die. Some species, such as Atlantic cod, have nearly been wiped out in this way.

We don't just take from the ocean, though: each year we dump 6.4 million tonnes of rubbish into it.

Factory waste oozing into a river

Nets with large holes let young fish go free.

Every year, an area of the world's forest larger than Hungary is chopped down.

Environmental disasters

Oil-soaked guillemot

Date	Location	Disaster
2002	Galicia, Spain	The *Prestige* oil spill. Over 900km of coastline polluted, and thousands of sea birds affected
2001	Galápagos islands	The *Jessica* oil spill. Many marine iguanas killed by oil pollution
1991	Kuwait	Oil fields set alight during the Gulf War, leading to air pollution and acid rain
1989	Alaska, USA	The *Exxon Valdez* oil spill. Many thousands of sea birds and animals killed by oil slick
1986	Chernobyl, Ukraine	Explosion of nuclear reactor. Thousands killed or damaged by radiation-related diseases
1984	Bhopal, India	Poison gas tank explosion. Over 8,000 people killed; thousands more disabled and injured

Uprooted

Forests act as a barrier to wind and water. Where trees are cut down, winds and floods can sweep away the soil, making the ground useless for growing anything at all.

Treeless land is unprotected.

Water woes

A fifth of all people don't have enough clean water to drink. Two-fifths have nowhere clean to go to the toilet.

Causes of water problems

- Rivers and seas polluted by chemical waste from factories
- Wasteful crop-watering methods
- Drought caused by global warming
- More people sharing water resources

Young girls collecting water from holes dug in the ground in Udaipur.

INTERNET LINKS
To find links to websites about Planet Earth's problems, go to **www.usborne-quicklinks.com**

Finding Solutions

Earth may have many problems, but it also has many people who are trying to solve them. Here are a few ways we can tackle some of Earth's problems.

Terrific terraces

Building terraces can stop heavy rain washing away soil from mountain slopes. For example, three rice crops a year can be grown on some terraces in Bali.

Rice has been farmed on terraces in Bali for hundreds of years.

Recycling

Many everyday items can be recycled. Here are just a few.

Cardboard boxes

Clothes

Electrical goods

Furniture

Glass jars and bottles

Magazines and papers

Metal drinks cans

Plastic bottles

Vegetable waste can be made into compost

This jacket began life as 25 plastic bottles.

Healthy mix

Soil can be made more fertile by growing different crops together, rather than only one. In Java, pineapples and winged beans are grown in alternate rows, which keeps the soil fertile.

Mixed crops keep soil tip-top.

Saving water

70% of the water we use in the world is used for watering crops. Spraying crops with water in hot areas is very wasteful because so much dries up in the Sun's heat.

A huge amount can be saved by giving plants small measures of water through holes in thin plastic tubes in the soil.

A wasteful way to water crops

Wind power

Electricity can be generated by wind turbines, rather than by burning fossil fuels in power stations.

If wind turbines were set up in the choppy seas around Great Britain, they could supply three times the power Britain uses today.

Just one wind turbine can supply the energy needs of 1,000 homes.

Tree bombs

One solution to the loss of forests is the amazing idea of dropping "tree bombs" from planes.

Stand clear!

Treeless areas could be bombed with thousands of saplings in cone-shaped capsules which would then rot and bed the trees into the earth.

In Japan and China, thousands of ducks are used, instead of dangerous chemicals, to control insects that attack rice fields. A duck can eat 2kg of insect pests a day.

Duck after a day's work

Sweet fuel

Many cars in Brazil run on fuel mixed with ethanol, made from sugar cane. Using ethanol causes less pollution than petrol.

Coral reefs shelter a huge range of sealife and are a barrier against strong waves.

INTERNET LINKS
To find links to websites about solving world problems, go to
www.usborne-quicklinks.com

Being prepared

Global warming* already seems to be bringing more natural disasters. Below are some actions that can be taken to reduce their effects.

Replant forests to protect soil from storms and floods

Use sensors and satellites to watch for early signs of disasters such as hurricanes

Limit the use of water, to protect against drought

Protect coral reefs, which defend shorelines from violent waves

*See page 50

Times and Seasons

The lengths of our days and years come from the time it takes the Earth to turn and to travel around the Sun.

Years and years

A year is the time it takes for the Earth to circle the Sun once. In the Gregorian calendar, a year has 365 days, but it actually takes the Earth 365.24 days to complete its circle.

To keep the calendar in step with the Sun, every fourth year has an extra day: February 29. These are called leap years. The maths still doesn't quite add up, though, so a leap year falling on a century is only counted as a leap year every 400 years.

INTERNET LINKS
To find links to websites about Earth's times and seasons, go to **www.usborne-quicklinks.com**

In each journey around the Sun, the Earth travels 940,000,000km.

Day and night

A day is the time it takes the Earth to spin once around on its axis: 24 hours. The half of the Earth facing the Sun has its daytime while the other half has its night.

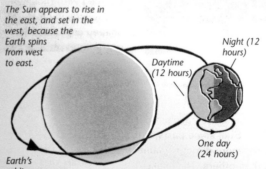

The Sun appears to rise in the east, and set in the west, because the Earth spins from west to east.

Daytime (12 hours)

Night (12 hours)

One day (24 hours)

Earth's orbit – one year

World calendars

Gregorian	Days	Jewish	Days	Islamic	Days	Indian	Days
Sun-based		*Sun- and Moon-based*		*Moon-based**		*Sun-based***	
January	31	Tishri (Sep-Oct)	30	Muharram	30	Chaitra (Mar-Apr)	30/31
February	28/29	Heshvan (Oct-Nov)	29/30	Safar	29	Vaishakha (Apr-May)	31
March	31	Kislev (Nov-Dec)	29/30	Rabi 1	30	Jyeshtha (May-Jun)	31
April	30	Tevet (Dec-Jan)	29	Rabi 2	29	Asadha (Jun-Jul)	31
May	31	Shevat (Jan-Feb)	30	Jumada 1	30	Shravana (Jul-Aug)	31
June	30	Adar 1 (Feb-Mar)	29	Jumada 2	29	Bhadra (Aug-Sep)	31
July	31	Adar 2 (in leap year)	30	Rajab	30	Ashvija (Sep-Oct)	30
August	31	Nisan (Mar-Apr)	30	Shaban	29	Kartika (Oct-Nov)	30
September	30	Iyar (Apr-May)	29	Ramadan	30	Agrahayana (Nov-Dec)	30
October	31	Sivan (May-Jun)	30	Shawwal	29	Pushya (Dec-Jan)	30
November	30	Tammuz (Jun-Jul)	29	Dhu al-Qadah	30	Magha (Jan-Feb)	30
December	31	Av (Jul-Aug)	30	Dhu al-Hijjah	29/30	Phalguna (Feb-Mar)	30
		Elul (Aug-Sep)	29				

* Being timed by moon cycles alone, Islamic months do not tie in with Gregorian months.
**This is the National Calendar of India. India also uses other Sun- and Moon-based calendars.

Be sure to pack your sunglasses if you're visiting the Arctic Circle this summer, because the Sun never sets during the summer months. The area inside the Circle is called the Land of the Midnight Sun.

Another sunny summer night in the Arctic circle...

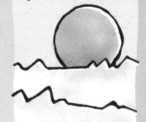

The seasons

The Earth is tilted at an angle. As it travels around the Sun, some parts of it get more direct sunlight than others. This makes the seasons change.

At the June solstice, when the Sun is overhead at the Tropic of Cancer, summer starts in the northern hemisphere and winter starts in the southern hemisphere. In December, the opposite happens.

At the equinoxes, the Sun is overhead at the equator. Neither hemisphere is then warmer than the other, and the milder seasons of spring and autumn begin.

Key
- Sun overhead
- Most direct sunlight
- Spring starts
- Summer starts
- Autumn starts
- Winter starts

March equinox
March 20 or 21
Day and night equal in length

June solstice
June 20 or 21
N. hemisphere: longest day
S. hemisphere: shortest day

December solstice
December 21 or 22
N. hemisphere: shortest day
S. hemisphere: longest day

September equinox
September 22 or 23
Day and night equal in length

55

World Records

This map shows where some of the highest, deepest, largest and longest features of Planet Earth are.

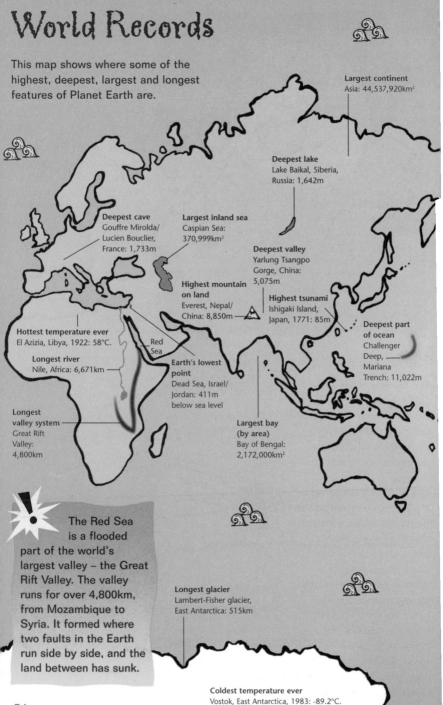

Largest continent
Asia: 44,537,920km²

Deepest lake
Lake Baikal, Siberia, Russia: 1,642m

Deepest cave
Gouffre Mirolda/ Lucien Bouclier, France: 1,733m

Largest inland sea
Caspian Sea: 370,999km²

Deepest valley
Yarlung Tsangpo Gorge, China: 5,075m

Highest mountain on land
Everest, Nepal/ China: 8,850m

Highest tsunami
Ishigaki Island, Japan, 1771: 85m

Deepest part of ocean
Challenger Deep, Mariana Trench: 11,022m

Hottest temperature ever
El Azizia, Libya, 1922: 58°C.

Red Sea

Longest river
Nile, Africa: 6,671km

Earth's lowest point
Dead Sea, Israel/ Jordan: 411m below sea level

Longest valley system
Great Rift Valley: 4,800km

Largest bay (by area)
Bay of Bengal: 2,172,000km²

The Red Sea is a flooded part of the world's largest valley – the Great Rift Valley. The valley runs for over 4,800km, from Mozambique to Syria. It formed where two faults in the Earth run side by side, and the land between has sunk.

Longest glacier
Lambert-Fisher glacier, East Antarctica: 515km

Coldest temperature ever
Vostok, East Antarctica, 1983: -89.2°C.

Largest ocean
Pacific Ocean:
155,557,000km²

Largest island
Greenland:
2,175,600km²

Longest fjord
Nordvest Fjord,
Scoresby Sund,
Greenland:
313km

**Largest bay
(by shoreline)**
Hudson Bay,
Canada: 12,268km

Highest geyser
Service Steamboat
Geyser, Yellowstone,
USA: 115m max.

Largest lake
Lake Superior,
USA/Canada:
82,414km²

Highest tide
Bay of Fundy, Nova
Scotia, Canada:
rises over 15m

**Highest
cliffs**
Molokai,
Hawaii
1,005m

Longest canyon
Grand Canyon,
Arizona, USA: 349km

Longest cave system
Mammoth Caves,
Kentucky, USA: 484km

Highest mountain on Earth
Mauna Kea, Hawaii: 10,203m
measured from seabed

Largest gulf
Gulf of Mexico:
1,544,000km²

Highest waterfall
Angel Falls,
Venezuela: 979m

**Highest seamount
(underwater volcano)**
near Tonga Trench:
8,690m

**Longest
mountain range**
Andes, South
America: 7,240km

Highest active volcano
Ojos del Salado, Chile/
Argentina: 6,887m

River carrying most water
Amazon, South America:
180,000m³ flows into the
Atlantic Ocean every second.

INTERNET LINKS
To find links to websites about Earth's amazing
features, go to **www.usborne-quicklinks.com**

Capital Cities

Country	Capital/s	Country	Capital/s
Afghanistan	Kabul	Denmark	Copenhagen
Albania	Tirana	Djibouti	Djibouti
Algeria	Algiers	Dominica	Roseau
Andorra	Andorra la Vella	Dominican Republic	Santo Domingo
Angola	Luanda	East Timor (Timor Leste)	Dili
Antigua & Barbuda	Saint John's	Ecuador	Quito
Argentina	Buenos Aires	Egypt	Cairo
Armenia	Yerevan	El Salvador	San Salvador
Australia	Canberra	Equatorial Guinea	Malabo
Austria	Vienna	Eritrea	Asmara
Azerbaijan	Baku	Estonia	Tallinn
Bahamas, The	Nassau	Ethiopia	Addis Ababa
Bahrain	Manama	Fiji	Suva
Bangladesh	Dhaka	Finland	Helsinki
Barbados	Bridgetown	France	Paris
Belarus	Minsk	Gabon	Libreville
Belgium	Brussels	Gambia, The	Banjul
Belize	Belmopan	Georgia	Tbilisi
Benin	Porto-Novo, Cotonou	Germany	Berlin
Bhutan	Thimphu	Ghana	Accra
Bolivia	La Paz, Sucre	Greece	Athens
Bosnia & Herzegovina	Sarajevo	Grenada	Saint George's
Botswana	Gaborone	Guatemala	Guatemala City
Brazil	Brasília	Guinea	Conakry
Brunei	Bandar Seri Begawan	Guinea-Bissau	Bissau
		Guyana	Georgetown
		Haiti	Port-au-Prince
Bulgaria	Sofia	Honduras	Tegucigalpa
Burkina Faso	Ouagadougou	Hungary	Budapest
Burma (Myanmar)	Rangoon	Iceland	Reykjavik
Burundi	Bujumbura	India	New Delhi
Cambodia	Phnom Penh	Indonesia	Jakarta
Cameroon	Yaoundé	Iran	Tehran
Canada	Ottawa	Iraq	Baghdad
Cape Verde	Praia	Ireland	Dublin
Central African Republic	Bangui	Israel	Jerusalem
Chad	Ndjamena	Italy	Rome
Chile	Santiago	Ivory Coast (Côte d'Ivoire)	Yamoussoukro
China	Beijing	Jamaica	Kingston
Colombia	Bogotá	Japan	Tokyo
Comoros	Moroni	Jordan	Amman
Congo	Brazzaville	Kazakhstan	Astana
Congo, Democratic Republic of	Kinshasa	Kenya	Nairobi
		Kiribati	Bairiki
Costa Rica	San José	Kuwait	Kuwait City
Croatia	Zagreb	Kyrgyzstan	Bishkek
Cuba	Havana	Laos	Vientiane
Cyprus	Nicosia	Latvia	Riga
Czech Republic	Prague	Lebanon	Beirut
		Lesotho	Maseru

Country	Capital/s	Country	Capital/s
Liberia	Monrovia	São Tomé & Príncipe	São Tomé
Libya	Tripoli	Saudi Arabia	Riyadh
Liechtenstein	Vaduz	Senegal	Dakar
Lithuania	Vilnius	Serbia & Montenegro	Belgrade
Luxembourg	Luxembourg	Seychelles	Victoria
Macedonia	Skopje	Sierra Leone	Freetown
Madagascar	Antananarivo	Singapore	Singapore
Malawi	Lilongwe	Slovakia	Bratislava
Malaysia	Kuala Lumpur	Slovenia	Ljubljana
Maldives	Malé	Solomon Islands	Honiara
Mali	Bamako	Somalia	Mogadishu
Malta	Valletta	South Africa	Cape Town,
Marshall Islands	Majuro		Pretoria,
Mauritania	Nouakchott		Bloemfontein
Mauritius	Port Louis	South Korea	Seoul
Mexico	Mexico City	Spain	Madrid
Micronesia,		Sri Lanka	Colombo, Sri
Federated States of	Palikir		Jayewardenepura
Moldova	Chisinau		Kotte
Monaco	Monaco	Sudan	Khartoum
Mongolia	Ulan Bator	Surinam	Paramaribo
Morocco	Rabat	Swaziland	Mbabane,
Mozambique	Maputo		Lobamba
Namibia	Windhoek	Sweden	Stockholm
Nauru	Yaren	Switzerland	Bern
Nepal	Kathmandu	Syria	Damascus
Netherlands	Amsterdam,	Taiwan	Taipei
	The Hague	Tajikistan	Dushanbe
New Zealand	Wellington	Tanzania	Dar es Salaam,
Nicaragua	Managua		Dodoma
Niger	Niamey	Thailand	Bangkok
Nigeria	Abuja	Togo	Lomé
North Korea	Pyongyang	Tonga	Nukualofa
Norway	Oslo	Trinidad & Tobago	Port-of-Spain
Oman	Muscat	Tunisia	Tunis
Pakistan	Islamabad	Turkey	Ankara
Palau	Koror	Turkmenistan	Ashkhabad
Panama	Panama City	Tuvalu	Funafuti
Papua New Guinea	Port Moresby	Uganda	Kampala
Paraguay	Asunción	Ukraine	Kiev
Peru	Lima	United Arab	
Philippines	Manila	Emirates	Abu Dhabi
Poland	Warsaw	United Kingdom	London
Portugal	Lisbon	United States	
Qatar	Doha	of America	Washington, D.C.
Romania	Bucharest	Uruguay	Montevideo
Russian Federation	Moscow	Uzbekistan	Tashkent
Rwanda	Kigali	Vanuatu	Porta-Vila
Saint Kitts & Nevis	Basseterre	Vatican City	Vatican City
Saint Lucia	Castries	Venezuela	Caracas
Saint Vincent &		Vietnam	Hanoi
the Grenadines	Kingstown	Yemen	Sana
Samoa	Apia	Zambia	Lusaka
San Marino	San Marino	Zimbabwe	Harare

Glossary

Arctic Circle The parallel (66°34′N) that circles the cold regions around the North Pole. In the northern summer the Sun never sets north of it.

Antarctic Circle The parallel (66°34′S) that circles the cold regions around the South Pole. In the southern summer the Sun never sets south of it.

Atmosphere A blanket of gases around a planet.

Axis An imaginary line through the Earth around which it spins.

Continental plate A tectonic plate supporting a land mass.

Continents Earth's great land masses: Asia, Africa, North and South America, Europe, Oceania (includes Australia) and Antarctica.

Crust Earth's rocky outermost layer.

Current A band of water running through the ocean.

Degree (°) Unit used to measure distance around the Earth as an angle of latitude or longitude.

Equator An imaginary circle, at 0° latitude, which divides the Earth into northern and southern hemispheres.

Equinoxes Days in March and September when the Sun is overhead at the equator and day and night are equal in length.

Erosion The process by which rock is worn down by wind and water.

Geologist Scientist who studies Earth's history, structure and rocks.

Hemisphere Half of the Earth, for example, the southern hemisphere.

International Date Line The meridian opposite the prime meridian. It snakes around 180° longitude, to avoid land. Places west of the line are a day ahead of those east of it.

Latitude Distance north or south, measured as an angle in degrees (°) from the equator.

Lava Liquid rock above the Earth's surface.

Lithosphere Earth's outer shell, made up of the crust and upper mantle.

Longitude Distance east or west, measured as an angle in degrees (°) from the prime meridian.

Magma Liquid rock under the Earth's surface.

Magnetic poles The two points on Earth's surface between which compass needles line up.

Mantle A hot, slowly shifting rock layer between the Earth's crust and core.

Meridians (lines of longitude) Imaginary lines joining the Earth's poles

Oceanic plate An undersea tectonic plate.

Parallels (lines of latitude) Imaginary circles around the Earth in line with the equator.

Poles Earth's geographic poles are the points at each end of its axis.

Prime meridian The meridian at 0° longitude, which passes through Greenwich, England.

Seamount A volcano beneath the sea surface.

Seaquake An undersea earthquake.

Solstices Days in June and December when the midday Sun is overhead at one of the Tropics.

Spreading ridge An undersea mountain range, formed when lava rises to fill cracks in the seabed.

Subduction zone A place where two plates collide and one plate moves beneath the other.

Tectonic plate A large piece of the Earth's lithosphere.

Trench A deep, V-shaped dip in the seabed, formed at a subduction zone.

Tropic of Cancer The most northerly parallel (23°26′N) at which the Sun is overhead in the northern summer.

Tropic of Capricorn The most southerly parallel (23°26′S) at which the Sun is overhead in the southern summer.

Using the Internet

Internet links

Most of the websites described in this book can be accessed with a standard home computer and an Internet browser (the software that enables you to display information from the Internet). We recommend:

• A PC with Microsoft® Windows 98 or later version, or a Macintosh computer with System 9.0 or later, and 64Mb RAM
• A browser such as Microsoft® Internet Explorer 5, or Netscape® 6, or later versions
• Connection to the Internet via a modem (preferably 56Kbps) or a faster digital or cable line
• An account with an Internet Service Provider (ISP)
• A sound card to hear sound files

Extras

Some websites need additional free programs, called plug-ins, to play sounds, or to show videos, animations or 3-D images. If you go to a site and you do not have the necessary plug-in, a message saying so will come up on the screen. There is usually a button on the site that you can click on to download the plug-in. Alternatively, go to www.usborne-quicklinks.com and click on Net Help. There you can find links to download plug-ins. Here is a list of plug-ins you might need:

RealOne™ Player – lets you play videos and hear sound files
QuickTime – lets you view video clips
Shockwave® – lets you play animations and interactive programs
Flash™ – lets you play animations

Help

For general help and advice on using the Internet, go to Usborne Quicklinks at www.usborne-quicklinks.com and click on Net Help. To find out more about how to use your web browser, click on Help at the top of the browser, and then choose Contents and Index. You'll find a huge searchable dictionary containing tips on how to find your way around the Internet.

Internet safety

Remember to follow the Internet safety guidelines at the front of this book. For more safety information, go to Usborne Quicklinks and click on Net Help.

Computer viruses

A computer virus is a program that can seriously damage your computer. A virus can get into your computer when you download programs from the Internet, or in an attachment (an extra file) that arrives with an email. We strongly recommend that you buy anti-virus software to protect your computer, and that you update the software regularly.

INTERNET LINK
To find a link to a website where you can find out more about computer viruses, go to www.usborne-quicklinks.com and click on Net Help.

Macintosh and QuickTime are trademarks of Apple Computer, Inc., registered in the U.S. and other countries.
RealOne Player is a trademark of RealNetworks, Inc., registered in the U.S. and other countries.
Flash and Shockwave are trademarks of Macromedia, Inc., registered in the U.S. and other countries.

Index

Acknowledgements

Every effort has been made to trace the copyright holders of the material in this book. If any rights have been omitted, the publishers offer to rectify this in any subsequent editions following notification. The publishers are grateful to the following organizations and individuals for their permission to reproduce material (t=top, m=middle, b=bottom, l=left, r=right):

Corbis: **1** Royalty-Free/CORBIS; **6** Myron Jay Dorf/CORBIS; **7** Bill Ross/CORBIS; **10br** Dewitt Jones/CORBIS; **12** S. P. Gillette/CORBIS; **15br** Tom Bean/CORBIS; **20m** Charles O'Rear/CORBIS; **21m** Bettmann/CORBIS, **21b** Roger Ressmeyer/CORBIS; **22b** Roger Ressmeyer/CORBIS; **24** Galen Rowell/CORBIS; **25** James Sparshatt/CORBIS; **29ml** Darrell Gulin/CORBIS; **38m** Graham Tim/CORBIS SYGMA; **39b** Nevada Weir/CORBIS; **41bm** Frederik Astier/CORBIS SYGMA; **45ml** Bettmann/CORBIS; **47m** Ralph A. Clevenger/CORBIS; **49ml** Chinch Gryniewicz, Ecoscene/CORBIS; **49r** Hans Strand/CORBIS; **50mr** Randy Wells/CORBIS
Courtesy Luca Pietranera, Telespazio, Rome, Italy: **36ml**
Courtesy Michael P. Frankis: **30bm**
Digital Vision: **10bl**; **11**; **13tr**, **br**; **22l**; **32br**; **35b**; **36bl**; **37tl**, **r**; **47b**; **50ml**, **b**; **51tr**, **ml**, **br**; **52bl**, **br**; **53ml**, **b**
Dr Ben Wigham/Ian Hudson, Southampton Oceanography Centre: **42bl**
Getty Images: **2-3** Getty Images/Richard Price; **31br** Getty Images/Darrell Gulin; **36br** Getty Images/Pete Turner; **37bm** Getty Images/William J. Hebert; **40** Getty Images/Erik Leigh Simmons; **46mr** Getty Images/Photodisc, **46b** Getty Images/Paul Souders; **51bl** Getty Images/Antonio M. Rosario
Science Photo Library: **17bl** Peter Menzel/Science Photo Library, **17br** Mark A. Schneider/Science Photo Library; **43bl** Dr Ken Macdonald/Science Photo Library
Historic Royal Palaces: **18bl** Crown copyright: Historic Royal Palaces. Reproduced by permission of Historic Royal Palaces under licence from the controller of Her Majesty's Stationery Office
James A. Pisarowicz PhD: **26mr**
Malcolm Walker, Royal MeteorologicalSociety: **12l**
National Aeronautics and Space Administration (NASA): **54t**
NASA/Goddard Spaceflight Center Scientific Visualization Studio: **45m**
National Oceanic and Atmospheric Administration (NOAA)/Dept of Commerce: **45b**
Natural History Picture Agency (NHPA): **26bl** NHPA/Stephen Krasemann
Richard D. Fisher: **27**
Robert M. Reed: **16tr**
U.S. Department of Interior/United States Geological Survey (USGS): **22r**, **23tm**, **tr**
US Navy: **44bl**
USGS: **13mr** USGS/Cascades Volcano Observatory, photographer: M. P. Doukas
www.patagonia.com: **52tr**

Illustrators Jerry Gower, Ian Jackson, Malcolm McGregor, Annabel Milne, Tricia Newell, Michelle Ross, Peter Stebbing, David Wright

Additional design Joanne Kirkby, Laura Hammonds, Candice Whatmore
Additional editing Sarah Khan, Elizabeth Dalby
Series editor Judy Tatchell